Pip By Pip: Forex Trading Strategies for the Winning Trader

Day Trading Strategies for the Smart Forex Trader

By: Donald Stanberry

I0510896

PUBLISHERS NOTES

Paperback Edition

Manufactured in the United States of America

DEDICATION

This book is dedicated to my parents. Without them I would not know how to work through the negative things in my life. I also learned that nothing is as simple as it seems- there is always a hidden challenge that has to be faced.

TABLE OF CONTENTS

CHAPTER 1- FOREX TRADING- AN INTRODUCTION

Do you wish to know how to trade Forex? If you're are a novice in the field of foreign exchange market trading, then you've certainly landed on the most informative and useful content there is online. Read on below as we discuss everything about Forex trading, from what the topic is all about, tips and guidelines on how to trade Forex correctly and so on.

How to Trade Forex

Before we guide you on how to trade Forex, let's first define what Forex trading is. You've probably heard of it from a friend or a colleague and that it is a lucrative field. This is true about foreign exchange trading, however, to reach that goldmine and start racking up huge amounts of income from your efforts, one should first be able to overcome all the obstacles and solve all the complexities that are present in the market. Basically, foreign exchange, also known as Forex, trading refers to the exchange of a particular currency for another. It is also defined as the conversion of one type of currency into another currency. The field refers to the international market in which currencies are traded virtually all day and night long. The term foreign exchange is typically called as Forex and in some cases FX.

Forex transactions cover everything from the conversion process of currencies, from a tourist at an airport stand to multi-million dollar payments made by large companies and governments in exchange for products and services that are imported from other countries. Consistently improving globalization has caused a colossal improvement in the amount of Forex transactions during the past few decades. The international Forex market is the biggest financial market at present, with an average regular volume amounting to trillions of dollars, $3.98 trillion to be exact. A huge portion of this value comes from spot transactions while the remaining percentage is directed in outright forwards, Forex swaps, currency swaps and options and other products.

There are several advantages on learning and mastering how to trade Forex rather than trade on stocks, futures, commodities or options. One major advantage of trading spot Forex is the bid and ask spread rates. Spread rates have drastically tightened in the past few years. Many internet-based Forex brokers and traders render a spread of 5 pips on European dollars, which is the most extensively traded and adaptive currency pair. Within the futures market, spreads can differ wildly anywhere between 5 and 9 pips and can become even bigger in terms of denser market conditions, which tend to occur importantly more often at futures currencies.

Another benefit of learning how to trade Forex is the margins requirements. Typically, a Forex trading with 1% margin is accessible. In simpler terms, this means that a trader can manage a

Donald Stanberry

position of a value of up to $1 million with nothing but $10,000 under his/her account. When compared, futures margins are not consistently altering, yet are also often predictable and measurable. Stocks are basically traded on a non-marginal basis and when they are, it can be limited up to half of the value.

Learning how to trade Forex and implementing it correctly will also yield the benefit of accessing a 24-hour market. Forex market trading happens round the clock. It starts at 24:00 CET in Asia on a Sunday evening and comes to a closing time on 23:00 CET in the US during Fridays. Though it is true that electronic communications networks are accessible for stock and futures markets that are responsible for supplying after-hours trading, liquidity is usually low and the costs rendered are of less quality and value.

Now going to the main question – how to trade Forex? Basically, the road to learning and mastering how to trade Forex begins with proper training. This is the key to emerging victorious over this fast-paced dynamic climate that the Forex market is surrounded with. Training on how to trade Forex usually comprises of enhancing your understanding of charts and Forex currency patterns, devising a Forex trading system that is effective and competitive, developing Forex forums and so on. Usually, training on how to trade Forex can go from as short as 6 months to as long as a full year. This time frame is recommended for novices in order to get the full grasp of the subject at hand.

Next step on how to trade Forex is to enter a Forex course. As you can imagine, the training opportunities are limitless and requires to be taken into serious consideration and be set with the appropriate precautionary measures. Everyone thinks that they have a system that works and that the system is ready to be shared publicly for a fixed fee. Regardless if it's the cheapest course you can find, fees will not dictate the competence and effectiveness of the Forex courses you're getting. Initiate your decisions on a Forex course succeeding your browsing of viable Forex trading sites and after you've learned and understood the basics without any costs involved.

The third step on how to trade Forex is Forex PIP. Learning and understanding the spread in foreign exchange and the pip of currency pairs will assist you in selecting an online Forex broker. You should make it a point to browse for Forex real-time quotes, which is vital if you are going to begin trading. The online marketplace is highly competitive thus researching thoroughly all trading platforms and online Forex brokers is crucial before you sign up.

Then, once you've learned how to trade Forex, you will now be trading online in a day-trading style. After you have cultivated a workable system and have set your stop losses into place, you will now have to understand charting and invest time on training so you can achieve a more solid foundation to start trading.

Overall, learning Forex trading is imperative if you want to succeed in the industry of foreign exchange market trading. How to trade Forex will require time and effort from you thus make sure you are absolutely certain that this is what you want. How to trade Forex is absolutely complex and challenging and even stressful at times, but once you get the hang of it, you can expect to reap huge amounts of benefits in the long run.

Chapter 2- Forex Robots

There is much information on how to get the best Forex robot today. However, it is never in your best interest to enter into any deal without putting several factors into consideration. Lots of fraudulent activities get played out both online and offline today concerning Forex robots. Anyone who does not look before he leaps is in for a really big show down in the hands of fraudsters. But you can be very sure that if you follow some very simple rules, you can be very sure of coming by something really worthy of note in terms of the best Forex robot. In case you are earnestly looking for a reliable Forex robot that will take your Forex trading experience to the very next level, this simple write up will give you some clues on how to make your search successfully.

Best Forex Robot

Don't Believe All You Read

While you are in search of the best Forex robot, you need to b very careful about what you believe. It is not all that you read online that can be relied upon. There is much unreliable info about Forex robots. While many sellers will claim theirs to be the best, you may end up discovering that such highly acclaimed robots are far from being reliable. Instead of taking their words for it, you will do well to find out from those who had used the robot before. This will help you to decide if it is the best Forex robot or not.

What Are The Reviews Saying?

You must never overlook the reviews while you are in search of the best Forex robot. The reviews can go a long way in determining how reliable or otherwise the robot is. Those who used the robot in times past will surely have one or two things to say about it. You can be very sure that whatever they have to say can be relied upon in making up your mind while searching for the best Forex robot. While following the reviews about the Forex robot, you still need to be very careful. This is because some online reviews about Forex robots can be stage managed in such a way that you will be deceived to believe in them. Make sure that you find out how reliable the site on which you are reading the reviews is before you follow the info therein.

What Are the Added Advantages?

Many Forex robots are designed today, and each of them can be applied differently. You should look out for a Forex robot that can work with the metatrader 4. This is the best Forex robot that anyone can ever come by. Metatrader 4 is actually the most widely used Forex trading platform all over the place. You should therefore ensure that the Forex robot is able to work on it before you consider it as the best Forex robot.

What Regulations Are Involved?

It is also important to find out if the Forex robot is properly regulated. This will surely ensure that it will give you the best of services that you are hoping for. A regulated Forex robot can surely be relied upon as the best Forex robot. If the robot is regulated, you will be sure that everything promised on the site making the robot available can be relied upon.

How Reliable Is the Customer Support

It may be somewhat impossible to come by a Forex robot that is completely reliable out there today; there will always be one gray area or the other. Every website providing Forex robot for sale should also give you access to reliable customer service. Before you can accept a robot as the best Forex robot, you need to find out if the site making it available is providing consistent customer service. Opt for anyone of them that is making support available to its clients for the 24 hours of the day.

How Adaptable Is the Robot

The adaptability of the robot can also give an indication into whether it is the best Forex robot or not. Make sure that the robot gives you an analysis on different charts; including hourly, daily, weekly, monthly and even yearly charts. Any Forex trading robot that does not give you such extended number of chart analysis may not be the best for your use.

Check Out the Price

Another factor that you should consider in your search for the best Forex robot is the issue of cost. While the Forex robot is designed to help you in making profit, it still should cost you something affordable. If the Forex robot costs you an arm and a leg, you should not consider it as the best Forex robot for you at all. There are so many good Forex trading robots out there that can be bought at very affordable price.

Caution While Trading

It is never in your best interest to completely rely on a Forex robot when you are carrying out your Forex trading. While it is true that the Forex robot can be very helpful in getting the work done, you should also realize that the Forex trading robot can misbehave. Some people make the mistake of leaving the Forex robot running on its own without proper monitoring. This is a very wrong way to make use of Forex robots. Even the best Forex robot needs to be properly monitored while it is carrying out trading processes. This will ensure that you do not end up losing your investment in Forex trading.

Pip by Pip

Any sincere maker of a Forex robot out there will tell you that Forex trading is not for everyone. However, it is possible for anyone to trade Forex these days due to the reliability of the Forex trading robots. If you are able to come by a very good Forex trading robot, you can be very sure that you will never have any problem in making very good sales out of your Forex trading endeavor. The best Forex robot will lead the way all through.

CHAPTER 3- ONLINE FOREX TRADING TIPS

Online Forex trading is an activity that is growing in popularity. It involves buying and selling different kinds of currency. Many people like to take part in Forex trading online because of the large earning potential. People like the idea of gaining thousands of dollars within a matter of weeks with very little work involved. Forex Trading is practice online globally. There are Forex Brokers all throughout the world in different countries. More people are becoming aware of this opportunity to earn money from their investment. There are a lot of neat tools and techniques that make trading a worthwhile activity.

Online Forex Trading

Pip by Pip

Online Forex trading has many different currency pairs. You have USD/JPY, EUR/USD, among many other pairs of currency. One of the most popular pairs of currency is EUR/USD. This is due to the fact that it is a fluid market. When you are trading Forex online, you have the chance of earning money a lot faster that investing in stocks and options. In this upset economy, people are looking for quick solutions to problems. Forex trading online represents that solution that many people are looking for.

In order to get started with Online Forex trading, you have to find a Forex broker. It is not a good idea to sign up with any Forex broker. There are certain steps that you must take in order to make sure that you are getting the best experience with Forex trading online. One important step is looking up customer reviews. There are a lot of sites that review Forex trading opportunities online. There are some sites out there that are willing to scam you. Also, some sites have Forex trading software that is faulty, which can ruin your chances of actually earning from Forex.

One feature that Online Forex trading sites have is leverage. With many sites, you can get up to 500:1 leverage which will enhance your earning potential. However, it is important to understand that with higher leverage, you can also lose a lot of money. Many people have lost tons of money from their over-leveraged accounts. A lot of people jump into Forex trading online with the wrong mindset. When trading Forex online, there are a lot of elements that you need to be aware of. One thing you need to look at is the forecasts. At the same time, you want to pay attention to any pattern that you might find with Forex.

A lot of people recommend that you start with a practice account first. Many Online Forex trading sites allow you to sign up for a demo account so that you can get a better idea of what to expect when you are participating in Forex trading online. Also, getting education on the markets would not hurt either. You shouldn't expect to get very far when trading Forex without sufficient knowledge. While nothing teaches like experience, learning from different sources can save you a lot of bumps and setbacks.

If you are using practice Online Forex trading account, you are probably wondering when you should open a live account. The best thing anyone can say is for you to open up an account when you feel comfortable. There is nothing that will guarantee you success. Even the most professional traders lose more often than they win. The best thing you can do is manage your losses so that you gain more than you lose. The Forex market is an unpredictable market. No matter what strategy you use when you are for Forex trading online, you are still more likely to lose than win.

In cases that you do lose, it is important not to get discouraged. It is also important not to get desperate. It is probably better for you to get discouraged than desperate because you can still walk away with what is left of your money depending on your losses. Desperation can cause you to lose a lot more money. Keep a cool head when you are trading. You do not want to allow emotions to get in the way. Forex trading online is a systematic exercise. Any anxieties and longings must be managed before taking part in trading. Think of it like being behind the wheel of a car while intoxicated.

When you decide to open up a live account, you should look for the requirements. Although many sites brokers have similar requirements, there are certain differing factors among each of them. One differing factor is the minimal amount needed to open up an account. Some brokers require you to have thousands of dollars before you can open up an account. There are others that will allow you to open up an account with $1 or even less. The

Pip by Pip

more respectable brokers will probably require a large amount of money to open with.

As you get into Forex Trading online, you do not want to bet more than you can afford to lose. The best thing to do is to start small. Bet small amounts without any leverage. As you get the feel of the activity, then you can advance to higher amounts. Even as you add to the amount, do not trade more than you can afford to lose. Many people have suffered devastating consequences out of neglect for this principle. Even if all of the signs point to a successful trade, you are still vulnerable to losing.

Online Forex trading is a double edged sword. While it can earn you a fortune, it can also break you completely. Success in the market involves a lot of studying and research. Above all, it involves commitment and wisdom. As you explore the world of Forex trading, listen to what other users have to say. One user described Forex trading as something that you do like a robot. Do not let emotions influence you. Just analyze the market and try to determine the right time to trade currency. Make your trade and wait. When the market is in your favor, then close the deal. While it is very rare to win big in Online Forex trading, you can at least manage your losses.

Are Forex Training Courses Necessary

The Forex training course is typically a four part program that teaches beginners how to participate in the world's largest business and succeed in it just like a professional. The Forex training course teaches the same techniques and trading methods that are used by hedge funds and banks and professional traders world-wide.

The Forex training course covers virtually every aspect of professional trading in a easy to follow, step by step guide because

Page | 16

who knows better than professional traders how confusing it can really be. Through a structured approach and a logical sequence through the core concepts learning the foundational element of professional trading anyone who really tries can achieve success.

What the best part is though, this eight week training course is done all online and can be done any day of the week and any hour of the day or night. By you setting your own schedule there is no rushing and your mind can concentrate on what is most important. That guarantees that you will get the most out of the training course and be able to trade with the professionals in no time.

In module one of the Forex training course you will learn all the essentials of Forex including a brief synopsis of why many traders fail and how to avoid those pitfalls. You will learn how to understand market conditions. You will learn all about high probability entry points and how important entry levels are when it comes to succeeding in the market. The psychology of trading is also a very important step that you will learn in week one. With the wrong mind frame no strategy or technique will ever work, this section focuses on how to avoid distractions and avoid impulsive behaviors. You will also learn how to plan your trades, the best currency pairs to trade, equity management and capital preservation.

By week two you will have learned the seven black and white strategies in trading and you will be learning about the "core four" or the Thinslice trading strategies. These strategies are vitally important because they occur on a daily basis in the Forex trading market. There is a high potential for profit when these strategies are used and you will learn how to use them to your advantage in easy to follow step by step instructions. You will also be taught the "final strategies" of Thinslice trading strategies. Even though the "final strategies" do not happen as often as the "core strategies"

Pip by Pip

they are just as powerful and precision is needed to work with them. All of these trading strategies will help you set up your own techniques in trading and will become an essential part of profiting in the trading market.

In module two of the Forex training course you will be observing all that you have learned previously and you will have a chance to see these strategies in action. In week four you will be attending a five hour live trading market session. Through this interactive training you will see how the concepts and strategies play out in a real time market. This part will be held through a web-cam conference so scheduling is still at your discretion. By week five you will be practicing how to identify and confirm the right entry point in the market.

In module three of the Forex training course you will have practice trading in live weekly sessions. In week six you will start trading using live capital to achieve the ten positive trades that are required.

In module four of the Forex training course you will learn chart patterns and this is where you are introduced to technical analysis indicators and there five basic categories. Week seven will include a scheduled support session with a one on one evaluation on the techniques you have learned. Through a web-cam conference a couple of your screenshots will be reviewed and your strategies will be discussed.

Refine or module number five is the final step in the Forex training course and the only one that is not done totally online. It will discuss trading styles such as day trading, scalping and swing trading; it will also discuss trading strategies such as pivots, breakout and patterns. The Forex training course also includes a two day on-site training class (in your nearest metropolitan area) where you will refine your own technique in trading. Seat reservation is required because it is a small group setting where questions can be asked and you will be walked through the whole process of live trading.

After becoming a member and completing the course you are never on your own. Membership also includes:

A direct email support line for any questions or concerns are answered usually within twelve hours and the support line is open twenty-four hours a day.

Approximately every two weeks (after completing the Forex training course) you will receive new members' articles and/or videos and any updates on the Forex training course.

After completing the Forex training course you will also have access to the live-trade setup forum where trading topics, price action strategies and the Forex training course are discussed.

There is also a daily posting of the Forex trade setup newsletter. You will find an analysis of at least two precious metals and five major Forex pairs. Any trend bias, key levels or price action setups that are relevant will also be posted.

It is guaranteed that after taking this course and learned the skill it takes anyone can be a Forex home-trader. Everyone learns at their own pace but this eight week Forex training course is designed for the beginner, in easy to understand terms and with graphs, charts and videos to help every step of the way. Most home-traders only work a couple of hours a day five days a week, that leaves the weekends free to do what you want. Even in today's economy after taking the Forex training course anybody can live the life of a professional trader.

Chapter 4- What are Forex Charts?

Forex trading is not a guessing game. It involves analysis of data and constant vigilance on the side of the trader in order to form an intelligent decision when it comes to making an investment. Traders often use a variety of tools and systems in order to help them determine the trends of the market. Using Forex charts is not uncommon as it helps in visualizing the trends and help traders quantify and understand the trends more accurately. Some of the most popular charts used by FX traders are the line, the bar and the candlestick.

The Line Chart

The line chart is the most basic of the three commonly used charts in Forex. Its name is derived from the series of interconnecting lines of data points formed by tracing the patterns of closing prices over a period of time. Relying on the line chart alone is not enough to make an accurate analysis, however, its strength as a tool is due to the clear visual it provides when it comes to data regarding closing prices from one period to another.

Determining the closing price is important for traders as it sets the value of a particular currency of a given market before trading starts again the next day at that same market. It can also be used to better understand the market sentiment on a given trading day by comparing it to the closing price of a previous date.

The Bar Chart

The bar chart is also known as the "OHLC" chart referring to the data displayed on the bar which are the open, high, low and close of a traded currency in a specific market in a given period of time. It is important to first determine the period covered on the chart in order to accurately understand the trend.

As opposed to the interconnected lines in the line chart, the bar chart is represented by vertical lines with horizontal dashes on each side. The topmost part of the bar represents the high. The dash on the upper part pointing to the right represents the close and the dash on the lower part pointing to the left is the open. The lowest part of the bar represents the low.

The advantage of the bar chart over the line chart is that it allows the trader to analyze not only the opening and closing of a currency price but the highs and lows as well.

The Candlestick Chart

Pip by Pip

The candlestick chart, also known as the Japanese candlestick chart is probably the most widely used of the three charts but also the most complicated. Its name was derived from its display representation which resembles an upright candlestick with the body representing the price opening and price closing and the wicks on both ends representing the highest price and the lowest price of the day respectively. The term Japanese implies its origin being the analysis tool used in Japanese trading since the 1700s.

The candlestick chart takes into consideration all the variables that are used in both the line and bar chart. In addition to these, it also includes in the analysis the emotion of traders as reflected on the data of a given trading day. As opposed to the other charts which analyze data of a given day's opening from the closing price of the previous day, the candlestick chart analyzes data from the opening of one particular trading day up to its closing. It also provides for a clearer visual as it uses a color coded approach in representing the uptrend and downtrend of the market.

Because of its combination approach in analyzing trends, it is thought to be the most accurate of the three commonly used chart analysis tools.

CHAPTER 5- FOREX TRADING SIGNALS

Forex trading is quite daunting and overwhelming even for the most experienced and skilled broker or trader. This being said, a beginner or novice in the field should expect to lose some money before they can really earn money from their Forex trading ventures. A novice in Forex trading will lack the skills and capabilities that are required to guarantee a profitable trade in the industry. In order to overcome these challenges, one has the option of learning and mastering it on their own.

Another problem when it comes to Forex Trading is that not everyone is able to commit their time in doing research and analysis over the vast stock market industry, which is a vital process that contributes to a successful investment. Fortunately, Forex trading signals are available in order to ensure maximum potential for profit. There are several Forex trading signals providers that are present today and offer signals for reasonable fees.

First, what does Forex trading signals system mean? Basically, it is a collection of analyses that any foreign exchange trader and broker utilize in order to identify when and what to buy and sell at a particular period of time. Forex signal systems can be based on technical scrutiny charting equipment or even news-based events. The day trader's currency trading system is typically composed of a multiplicity of signals that operate in sync to come up with a buy and sell decision. Forex trading signals are accessible for an affordable charge while some even come for free. Meanwhile those who are experienced and versed enough usually decide to develop their own signal systems themselves in order to save money as well as use the skill to profit from it.

Moreover, Forex trading signals can produce executions that can either be manual or automated. A manually set system comprises of a trader sitting in front of the computer and personally looking for signals while interpreting the results on which he/she will base whether to buy or sell. Meanwhile, automated trading systems comprise of a trader setting the software with commands on what signals to search for and how these will be interpreted.

Both manual and automated Forex trading signals are accessible for purchase online. However, it is important to take note that there is no such thing as the perfect trading signal. If there was a system that came near to a perfect trading signal, the developer or seller won't want to share it. This is the very reason why large financial corporations keep their "black box" trading software products privatized.

There are a multitude of benefits that are entailed by incorporating trading signals into your Forex trading venture. One is that you are able to save significant amounts of time from focusing and spending countless hours in front of the computer screen and manually managing your accounts and looking for valuable signals.

The system requires only around 10 minutes of your time a day and you can head on doing what you want, whether it be shopping, playing sports or spending the day to relax and sleep. When you use a Forex trading signal provider, you will only need to follow the signals at a set period of time per day. With this, the learning curve is shortened and you are spared from all the stressful and complex obstacles and challenges. This may be the best advantage of Forex trading signals yet. There is no need to invest your time on learning on how the market works.

Another benefit of the service is that you can lower the risks that are involved in the currency trading. Starting out as a novice, all aspects of trading become risky mainly due to the fact that the

Donald Stanberry

individual lacks the knowledge and skills. This is a perfect feature and a plus for novices who don't want to risk too much of their money when venturing into the complex world of Forex trading.

Users of the system are also able to obtain valuable information regarding Forex alterations quickly and be able to grasp the foreign exchange market easily. Given fast and reliable information, even a novice can execute buying and selling decisions instantaneously. Immediate actions are important, especially for stock exchange market wherein rates tend to change rapidly. Lastly, given time and commitment in practicing the system, traders can discover more benefits and features that can be applied in order to make their responsibilities much less complex and much more profitable.

So how do you find and invest on the best Forex trading signals provider? One thing you should remember is that basing your decision on the best Forex trading signals provider through the previous displayed results is wrong. This is a common mistake for most shoppers of Forex trading signals systems. Recent results are not as vital as you may think it to be. This is mainly due to the fact that the recent results will not dictate the performance of the system for the long run.

One major factor that contributes to a good Forex trading signals provider is the developer. A software program is only as good as its developer. You should research thoroughly about the developer's background; his/her credentials and other pertinent data that may help you determine whether the developer is competent and reliable or just a scam artist trying to get your money.

Overall, employing Forex trading signals for your business endeavors will play a vital role towards success as well as give you a competitive edge against other stock traders and brokers. Forex trading signals are definitely a heaven sent for Forex trading participants; when purchasing Forex trading signals always

Pip by Pip
remember to be wise and patient to avoid wasting valuable resources.

CHAPTER 6- DAY TRADING-FOREX

As you have garnered from the previous chapters, Forex day trading has become important in the modern business world. In the past, every country had self-sufficient economies, and international trading was very much important. But today, the picture has totally changed, international trading has become very important and today the power of each country is determined by the size of their share in the international economy. So the competition to increase international trading is very high among countries. And since international trading exchanging of foreign currencies has become so important, it has lead to Forex day trading.

Forex Day Trading

In this context, Forex day trading plays a very important role and it can be defined like this. Foreign exchange, also known as FOREX for short, is an activity wherein money of one country is exchanged for the currency of another; and in this task, financial gain can be obtained with the differences of buying and selling of currencies.

Pip by Pip

Though it is a risky business, considerable profits can be generated and an accurate evaluation of the situation of the market is very important for this business to succeed.

Trading styles can be categorized by length of time between initial and offsetting trade. Short, medium and long-term trades can be executed. Day trading means offsetting a trade within a day's trading session.

The most important activity that can happen through Forex Trading is that through the help of the fluctuations in exchange rates of different countries, one can invest in Speculation and Arbitrage. Both of these activities are related to an exchange rate system. And Forex Trading is the best option for anyone to invest its money and earn huge profits through exchange rate fluctuations. There are many other business opportunities for investors to earn money through Forex Day Trading.

There are plenty of different benefits available to those who are finally moving into the world of Forex trading. The system simply provides people with a means that they can actively invest their money in, and do this in a unique and interesting way. With that being said, there are some negatives to the world of Forex day trading. Those who are curious about entering this market are going to want to consider both the good and the bad before entering the system.

As many benefits of Foreign exchange day trading are available, people take interest on it. As the demand has gone up, many software tools are developed and money can be invested to gain profits. With the help of deeply considering the pros and cons of Foreign exchange Day Trading, one can understand the working and benefits of Forex trading in depth. There are some positive points of it that would compel you to start buying and selling at Foreign exchange Trading. Along with these positive points, some are its flaws that must be minimized and keep in consideration while doing trading through it. However both advantages and disadvantages are available in Foreign exchange day trading and some of them are identified below.

Easily Start Trading

Anyone can start it as a business if access to the internet is available, no matter where you are. You can earn money by doing Forex day trading transactions. Most importantly time is also not a barrier as this Forex day trading business can be done throughout the day.

Higher Leverage

Though you have small margin deposits, large profit can be expected from Foreign exchange day trading as large leverage is provided to the traders.

Depend On the Conditions of Economy

Forex is totally dependent on the conditions of the economy. If better news has arrived, you are able to obtain better position in the trading market; so that it can be stated that Forex day trading can be profitable based on reactions of the market.

Stop Loss Tools Are Available

Many stop loss tools are available for Forex day trading, and can be used to determine the amount you're willing to lose. This could help reducing huge losses in the Forex day trading market.

Availability of Different Software Applications

Pip by Pip

Various software applications which are designed for Forex day trading are available now so that individuals can enter the market easily. Different analyzing tools are integrated to these software products which enhance customer awareness about Forex day trading.

People who join the trading markets and run their business are totally dependent on the software, hardware and network connections. A breakdown of servers or internet connectivity may damage the business greatly.

Large leverage might be a risk as corresponding danger of getting into positions which pose huge risk on the size of accounts. Good capital management skills should be used.

If bad news were to arrive, a market could move against you. Therefore it is a must to analyze each situation of the market and examine the reactions for different scenarios of the economies to prevent losses.

Though stop loss tools are available, traders can be greedy aiming to amass huge profits- on the other hand, over confidence can be built on stop loss tools, and this may lead to considerable losses.

Alternative investment options are available and money can be invested on these investment options.

Foreign exchange day trading has very complex procedures. New investors may be reluctant to enter the market and may find it hard to survive long term.

Managing personal finance is not easy task and Forex day trading is one of the best investing options available in the world. Most importantly it is one of easiest methods for earning money as it is flexible enough to operate twenty four hours. Many people use

Donald Stanberry

this method to gain profits and it can be noted that various facilities are available for investors such as specially designed software tools and applications among others.

Forex day trading is totally linked with the situation of the economy and it can be stated that it can be a gold mine, if you can play correctly as there are risks and dangers involved. Forex day trading can be rewarding and exciting, as long as you cover your bases!

CHAPTER 7- WHY DO FOREX TRADING AT HOME

When people ask me what I do for a living, and I respond with an answer like, "I'm a work at home Forex trader", the response I get is usually some variant on "huh?" It seems that most people have never even heard of "Forex trading", let alone know that it is a viable career option in the twenty-first century.

I was at a party last week with my wife, and a gentleman I met that evening asked me the same question. When I told him what my other occupation was, he asked me, "oh, is that like the stock market?" I said in general, yes, but simpler.

Most people only think about different currencies when they are taking a vacation and need to exchange money, or making a purchase online from a different country. They are completely unaware that currency trading is a multi-trillion dollar industry that anyone with a computer and a high-speed internet connection can get involved in. But to be fair, up until about 2 years ago, I didn't really know anything about Forex trading either.

So in that spirit, here is my list of the top reasons I trade Forex from home!

Profit

The money — obviously, the number one reason I love to trade Forex. Trading Forex pays my mortgage, paid for my new car, our recent home renovations, and many other things that contribute to my quality of life.

Comfort, Flexibility and Freedom

Trading Forex allows me to work when I want, where I want, and how I want. The global currency market runs 24 hours a day — so I can trade whenever it is most convenient for me. If I have a late night out, I can sleep in and work a little bit later in the evening. If I have things to do during the day, I can work around them. If I have things to do during the week, I can work on the weekend. I can also trade in my pajamas! And since everything is online, I can trade from wherever I am in the world — all I need is a laptop and an internet connection.

Excitement

I can't deny it — I get a rush from trading.

ABOUT THE AUTHOR

Donald Stanberry was a pre-school teacher who simply had to find a way to make more money to support his family. His wife was recovering from major surgery and he had to double up to keep up with the bills. When he thought that the debt and bills would bury him, he found out about Forex trading. It was new and scary to him but he found that as long as he stuck to the rules and kept abreast of changes he could earn enough to supplement his income.

From his experience, he wrote a book on the subject. It is a guide for others who may have heard about it but are afraid to trade as they are afraid to lose the little money they do have. Donald informs, educates and reassures his readers of the benefits of trading.

www.ingramcontent.com/pod-product-compliance
Lightning Source LLC
Chambersburg PA
CBHW051305170526
45165CB00004B/1864